FAVORITE CHRISTMAS CAROLS
FOR CLASSICAL PLAYERS

To access recorded piano accompaniments online, visit:
www.halleonard.com/mylibrary

Enter Code
2553-7457-0083-1712

ISBN 978-1-5400-2979-9

Visit Hal Leonard Online at
www.halleonard.com

Contact Us:
Hal Leonard
7777 West Bluemound Road
Milwaukee, WI 53213
Email: info@halleonard.com

In Europe, contact:
Hal Leonard Europe Limited
42 Wigmore Street
Marylebone, London, W1U 2RN
Email: info@halleonardeurope.com

In Australia contact:
Hal Leonard Australia Pty. Ltd.
4 Lentara Court
Cheltenham, Victoria, 3192 Australia
Email: info@halleonard.com.au

HOW TO USE HAL LEONARD ONLINE AUDIO

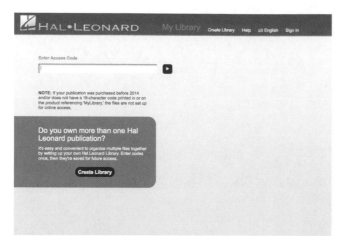

Because of the changing use of media, and the fact that fewer people are using CDs, we have made a shift to companion audio accessible online. In many cases, rather than a book with CD, we now have a book with an access code for online audio, including performances, accompaniments or diction lessons. Each copy of each book has a unique access code. We call this Hal Leonard created system "My Library." It's simple to use.

Go to www.halleonard.com/mylibrary and enter the unique access code found on page one of a relevant book/audio package.

The audio tracks can be streamed or downloaded. If you download the tracks on your computer, you can add the files to a CD or to your digital music library, and use them anywhere without being online. See below for comments about Apple and Android mobile devices.

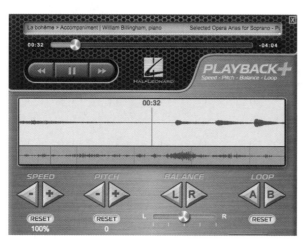

There are some great benefits to the My Library system. *Playback+* is exclusive to Hal Leonard, and when connected to the Internet with this multi-functional audio player you can:

• Change tempo without changing pitch
• Transpose to any key

Optionally, you can create a My Library account, and store all the companion audio you have purchased there. Access your account online at any time, from any device, by logging into your account at www.halleonard.com/mylibrary. Technical help may be found at www.halleonard.com/mylibrary/help/

Apple/iOS

Question: On my iPad and iPhone, the Download links just open another browser tab and play the track. How come this doesn't really download?

Answer: The Safari iOS browser will not allow you to download audio files directly in iTunes or other apps. There are several ways to work around this:

• You can download normally on your desktop computer, saving the files to iTunes. Then, you can sync your iOS device directly to your computer, or sync your iTunes content using an iCloud account.

• There are many third-party apps which allow you to download files from websites into the app's own file manager for easy retrieval and playback.

Android

Files are always downloaded to the same location, which is a folder usually called "Downloads" (this may vary slightly depending on what browser is used (Chrome, Firefox, etc)). Chrome uses a system app called "Downloads" where files can be accessed at any time. Firefox and some other browsers store downloaded files within a "Downloads" folder in the browser itself.

Recently-downloaded files can be accessed from the Notification bar; swiping down will show the downloaded files as a new "card", which you tap on to open. Opening a file depends on what apps are installed on the Android device. Audio files are opened in the device's default audio app. If a file type does not have a default app assigned to it, the Android system alerts the user.

CONTENTS

Pianists on the recordings: [1] Brendan Fox, [2] Richard Walters

The price of this publication includes access to companion recorded piano accompaniments online,
for download or for streaming, using the unique code found on the title page.
Visit www.halleonard.com/mylibrary and enter the access code.

Angels We Have Heard on High

Traditional French Carol
Arranged by Joshua Parman

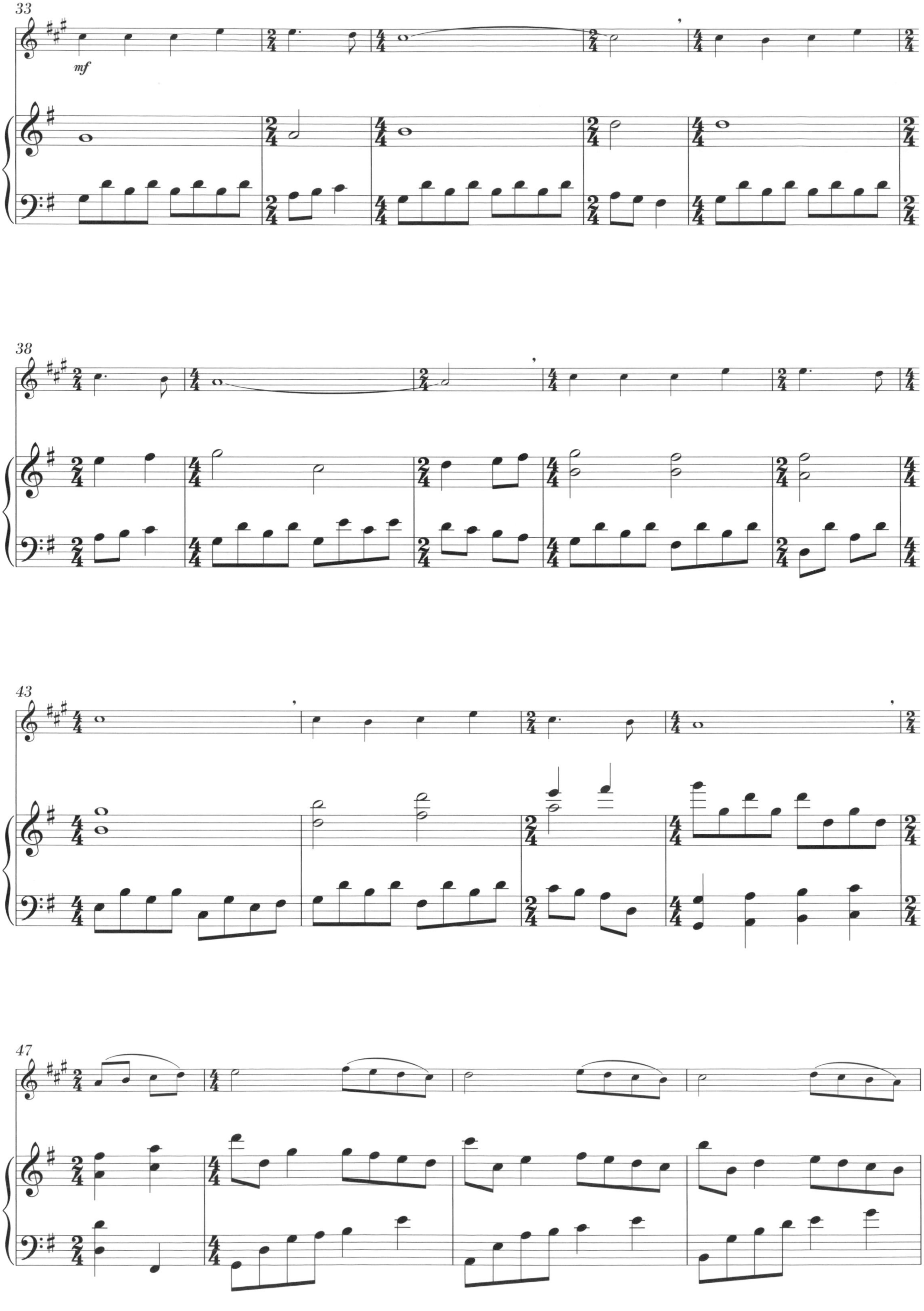
33
mf
38
43
47

Away in a Manger

William J. Kirkpatrick
Adapted from an arrangement
by Christopher Ruck

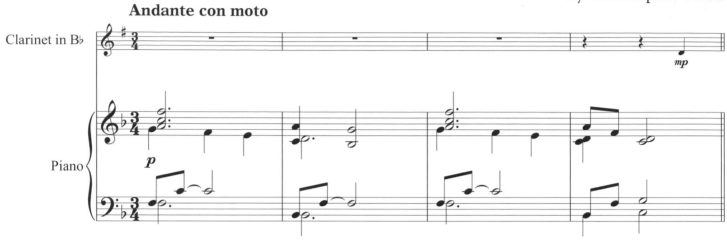

Coventry Carol

English Melody
Arranged by Joel K. Boyd

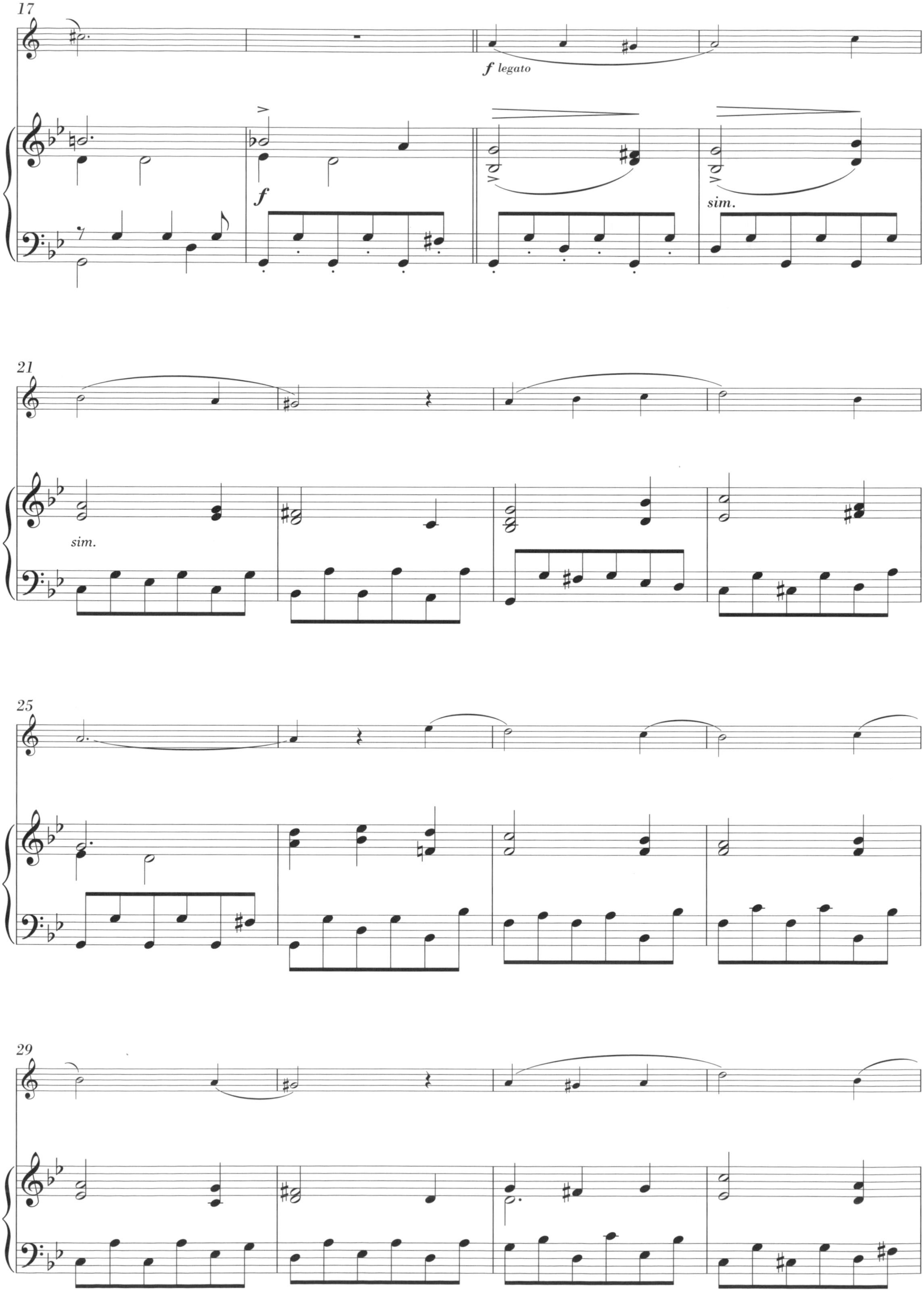
17
f legato
f
sim.
21
sim.
25
29

Deck the Hall

Traditional Welsh Carol
Arranged by Richard Walters

The First Noel

Traditional English Carol
Arranged by Joel K. Boyd

This page has been intentionally left blank to facilitate page turns.

God Rest Ye Merry, Gentlemen

Traditional English Melody
Arranged by Brendan Fox

He Is Born

18th century French Carol
Adapted from an arrangement
by Brian Dean

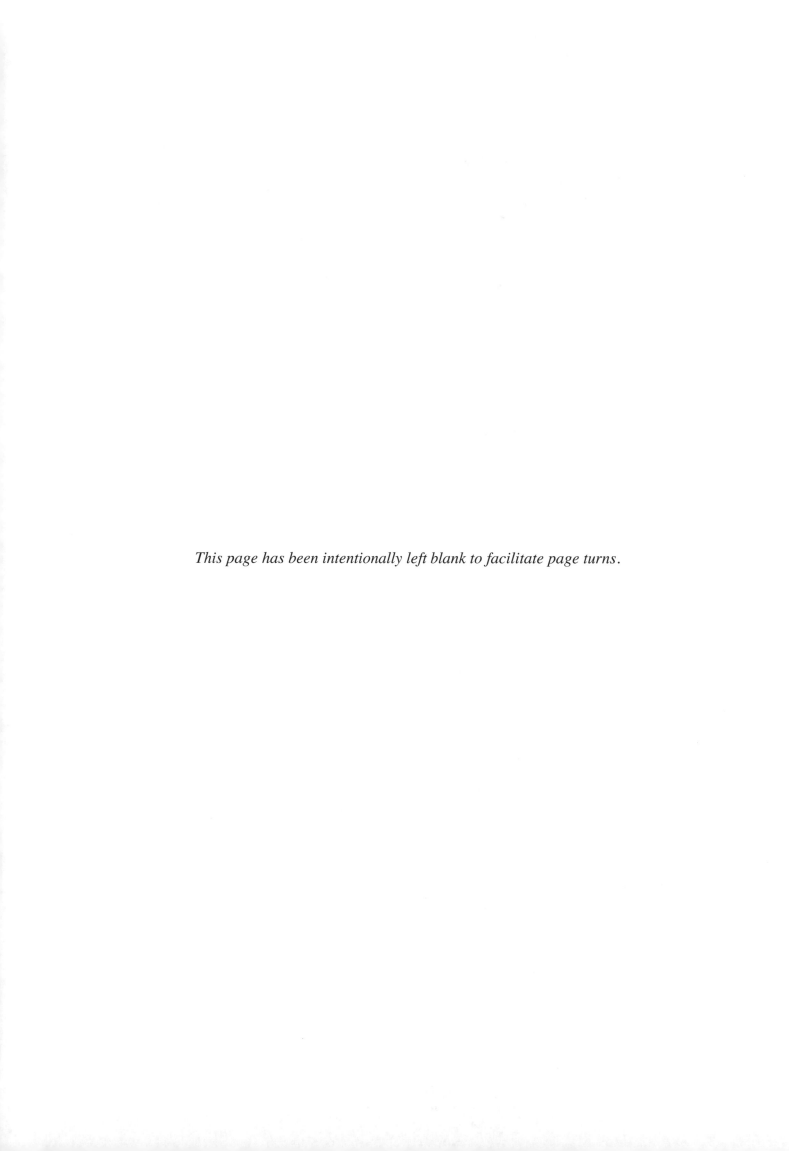

This page has been intentionally left blank to facilitate page turns.

In dulci jubilo

German Carol, 14th century
Arranged by Richard Walters

In the Bleak Midwinter

Gustav Holst
Adapted from an arrangement
by Brian Dean

This page has been intentionally left blank to facilitate page turns.

Infant Holy, Infant Lowly

Polish Carol
Adapted from an arrangement
by Christopher Ruck

FAVORITE CHRISTMAS CAROLS
FOR CLASSICAL PLAYERS

To access recorded piano accompaniments online, visit:
www.halleonard.com/mylibrary

Enter Code
5074-8174-1335-7483

ISBN 978-1-5400-2979-9

HAL•LEONARD®

Visit Hal Leonard Online at
www.halleonard.com

Contact Us:
Hal Leonard
7777 West Bluemound Road
Milwaukee, WI 53213
Email: info@halleonard.com

In Europe, contact:
Hal Leonard Europe Limited
42 Wigmore Street
Marylebone, London, W1U 2RN
Email: info@halleonardeurope.com

In Australia contact:
Hal Leonard Australia Pty. Ltd.
4 Lentara Court
Cheltenham, Victoria, 3192 Australia
Email: info@halleonard.com.au

HOW TO USE HAL LEONARD ONLINE AUDIO

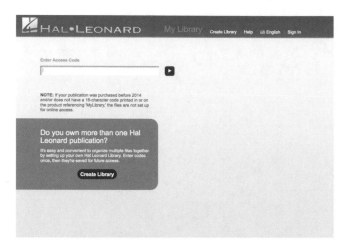

Because of the changing use of media, and the fact that fewer people are using CDs, we have made a shift to companion audio accessible online. In many cases, rather than a book with CD, we now have a book with an access code for online audio, including performances, accompaniments or diction lessons. Each copy of each book has a unique access code. We call this Hal Leonard created system "My Library." It's simple to use.

Go to www.halleonard.com/mylibrary and enter the unique access code found on page one of a relevant book/audio package.

The audio tracks can be streamed or downloaded. If you download the tracks on your computer, you can add the files to a CD or to your digital music library, and use them anywhere without being online. See below for comments about Apple and Android mobile devices.

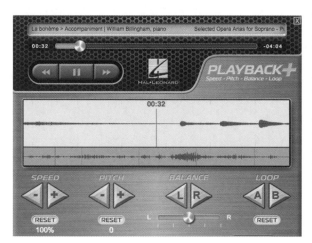

There are some great benefits to the My Library system. *Playback+* is exclusive to Hal Leonard, and when connected to the Internet with this multi-functional audio player you can:

• Change tempo without changing pitch
• Transpose to any key

Optionally, you can create a My Library account, and store all the companion audio you have purchased there. Access your account online at any time, from any device, by logging into your account at www.halleonard.com/mylibrary. Technical help may be found at www.halleonard.com/mylibrary/help/

Apple/iOS

Question: On my iPad and iPhone, the Download links just open another browser tab and play the track. How come this doesn't really download?

Answer: The Safari iOS browser will not allow you to download audio files directly in iTunes or other apps. There are several ways to work around this:

• You can download normally on your desktop computer, saving the files to iTunes. Then, you can sync your iOS device directly to your computer, or sync your iTunes content using an iCloud account.

• There are many third-party apps which allow you to download files from websites into the app's own file manager for easy retrieval and playback.

Android

Files are always downloaded to the same location, which is a folder usually called "Downloads" (this may vary slightly depending on what browser is used (Chrome, Firefox, etc)). Chrome uses a system app called "Downloads" where files can be accessed at any time. Firefox and some other browsers store downloaded files within a "Downloads" folder in the browser itself.

Recently-downloaded files can be accessed from the Notification bar; swiping down will show the downloaded files as a new "card", which you tap on to open. Opening a file depends on what apps are installed on the Android device. Audio files are opened in the device's default audio app. If a file type does not have a default app assigned to it, the Android system alerts the user.

CONTENTS

Pianists on the recordings: [1] Brendan Fox, [2] Richard Walters

The price of this publication includes access to companion recorded piano accompaniments online,
for download or for streaming, using the unique code found on the title page.
Visit **www.halleonard.com/mylibrary** and enter the access code.

Angels We Have Heard on High

Traditional French Carol
Arranged by Joshua Parman

Away in a Manger

William J. Kirkpatrick
Adapted from an arrangement
by Christopher Ruck

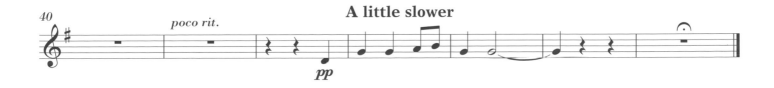

Coventry Carol

English Melody
Arranged by Joel K. Boyd

Deck the Hall

Traditional Welsh Carol
Arranged by Richard Walters

The First Noel

Traditional English Carol
Arranged by Joel K. Boyd

God Rest Ye Merry, Gentlemen

Traditional English Melody
Arranged by Brendan Fox

He Is Born

18th century French Carol
Adapted from an arrangement
by Brian Dean

In dulci jubilo

German Carol, 14th century
Arranged by Richard Walters

In the Bleak Midwinter

Gustav Holst
Adapted from an arrangement
by Brian Dean

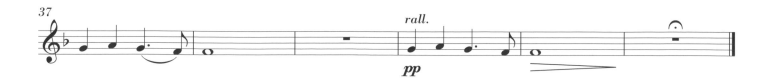

Infant Holy, Infant Lowly

Polish Carol
Adapted from an arrangement
by Christopher Ruck

14

Joy to the World

George Frideric Handel
Arranged by Brendan Fox

Lo, How a Rose E'er Blooming

Traditional German Carol
From *Kölner Gesangbuch*, 1599
Arranged by Richard Walters

O Come, All Ye Faithful
(Adeste Fideles)

John Francis Wade
Arranged by Joshua Parman

O Come, O Come Emmanuel

French Melody, 15th century
Arranged by Richard Walters

O Holy Night

Adolphe Adam
Transcribed by Celeste Avery

Once in Royal David's City

Henry J. Gauntlet
Arranged by Richard Walters

Silent Night

Franz X. Gruber
Arranged by Brendan Fox

Still, Still, Still

Traditional Austrian Carol
Adapted from an arrangement
by Brian Dean

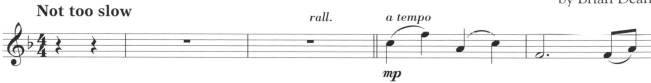

Sussex Carol

Traditional English Carol
Adapted from an arrangement
by Christopher Ruck

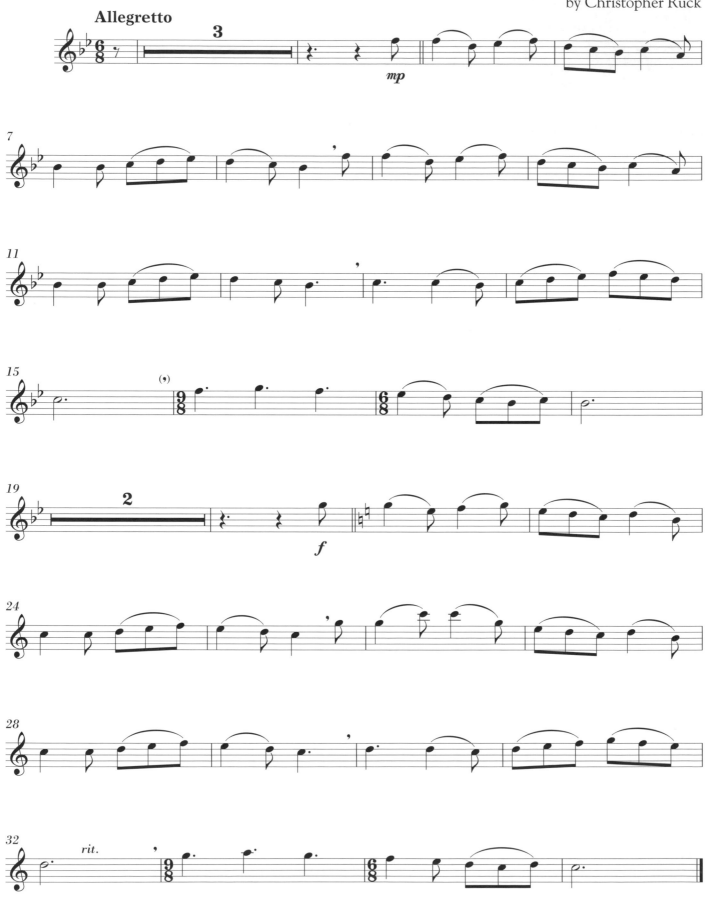

What Child Is This?

16th century English Folksong
Adapted from an arrangement
by Bryan Stanley

Joy to the World

George Frideric Handel
Arranged by Brendan Fox

Lo, How a Rose E'er Blooming

Traditional German Carol
From *Kölner Gesangbuch*, 1599
Arranged by Richard Walters

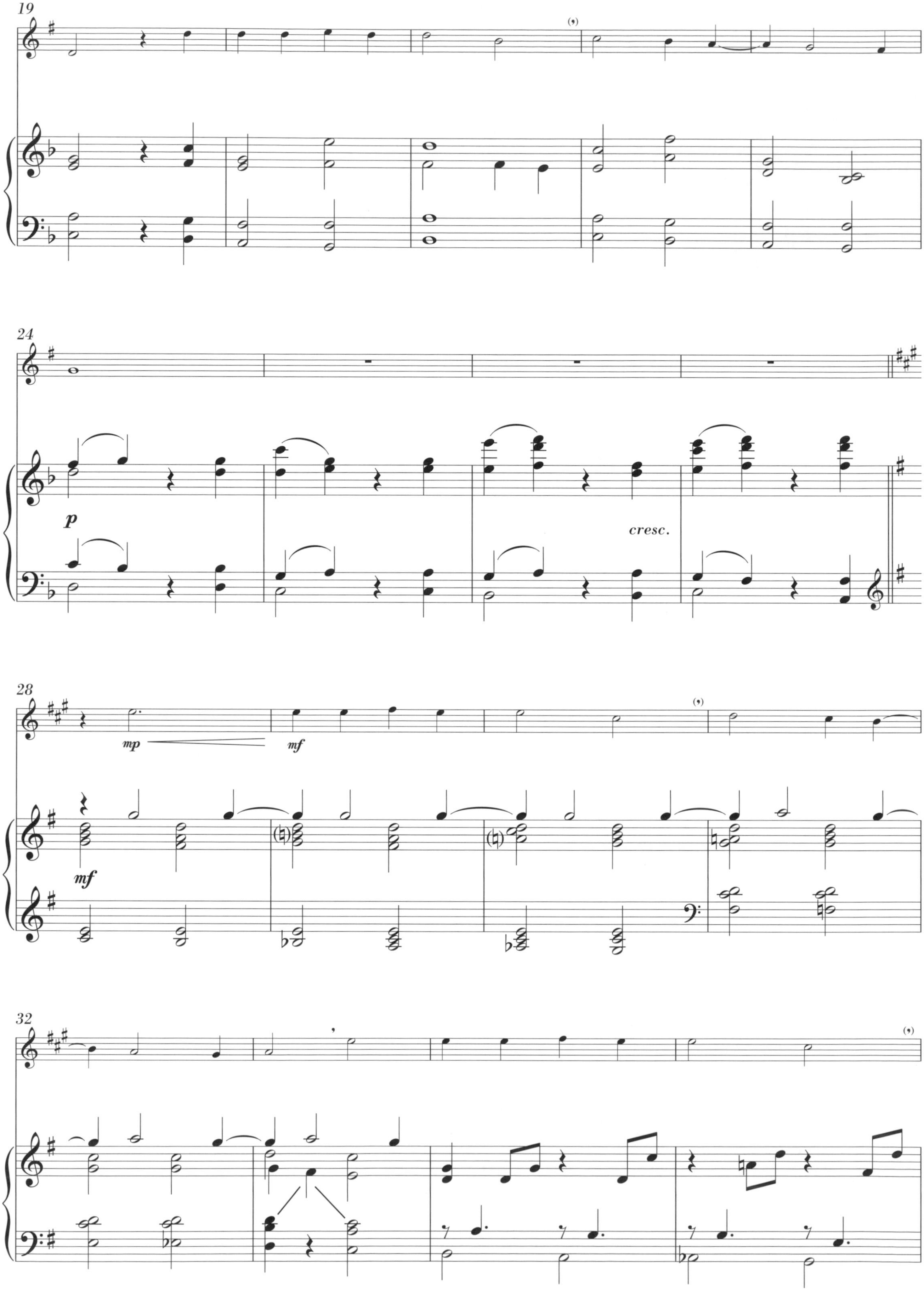
19
24
p
cresc.
28
mp
mf
mf
32

O Come, All Ye Faithful
(Adeste Fideles)

John Francis Wade
Arranged by Joshua Parman

O Come, O Come Emmanuel

French Melody, 15th century
Arranged by Richard Walters

O Holy Night

Adolphe Adam
Transcribed by Celeste Avery

Once in Royal David's City

Henry J. Gauntlet
Arranged by Richard Walters

This page has been intentionally left blank to facilitate page turns.

Silent Night

Franz X. Gruber
Arranged by Brendan Fox

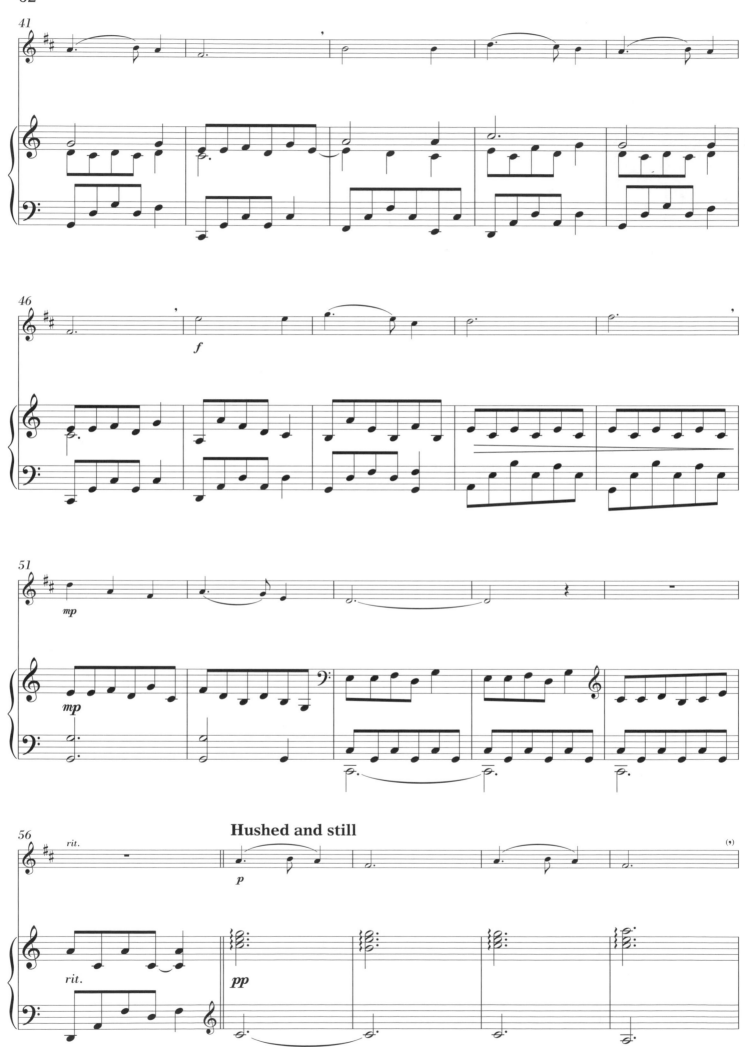

Still, Still, Still

Traditional Austrian Carol
Adapted from an arrangement
by Brian Dean

Sussex Carol

Traditional English Carol
Adapted from an arrangement
by Christopher Ruck

What Child Is This?

16th century English Folksong
Adapted from an arrangement
by Bryan Stanley